A Basic Guide To Podcasting

Davo Roberts

A Basic Guide To Podcasting

Davo Roberts

With
Alphy the WOWChurch Cat
And Guest Podcaster,
Drongo Davo

Acknowledgements

What's It All About, Alphy? A Basic Podcasting Guide– version 1.0

Text & Graphics Copyright © 2022 Dave G Roberts

ISBN: 9798844635779

Also available in full colour on Kindle

Dedication

Firstly, to the Lord our God – Father, Son and Holy Spirit. I wouldn't be here without Him.

Secondly to my wife, Youngmi. She is my one and my only. I can't imagine life without her and I thank God for her daily.

Roger Kirby, who was mentor, editor, but most of all, good friend. He was willing to learn about Podcasting. He fought the good fight and is now in the presence of His Saviour, Jesus Christ.

Finally, to the listeners of our podcasts globally. Thank you!

Contents

Introduction

G'day! Alphy the WOWChurch Cat here again!

I have a friend with me! Say hello to the Rev Drongo Davo!

Thanks Alphy, me little bonza Cat!

G'day mates!

We are going to introduce the basics of the world of Podcasts.

PODCASTS

1. Getting Started

2. Recording

Here we go.

Let's start with the basic equipment you will need to start off with.

You will need obviously some form of recording device.

That could be a computer, laptop, phone or tablet with a wired or Bluetooth microphone.

Ideally an external microphone with a Pop Screen to give a better quality recording.

The Microphone Pop Screen is a noise protection filter between you and your microphone. It is the orange line on the microphone here.

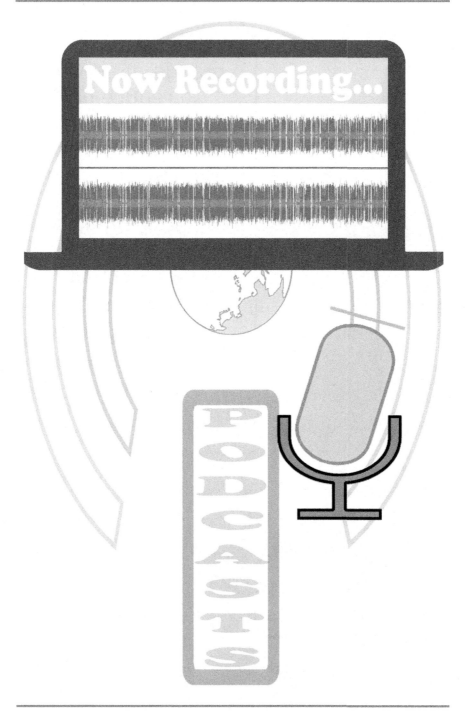

3. Recording Software

Recording In Progress

Press Here To Stop Recording

The computer or device will need recording software or recording app.

This will also allow you to both record and edit your Podcast.

I use this app, which is Audacity, and it will run on your Windows or Apple Computer.

It is open source and free.

Of course, there are other programs and apps also available.

4. Meta Tags

As you save your Podcast before uploading to your Podcast Host, ensure that you change the Meta Tag info.

A Meta tag is the identifying information associated with each of your Podcast files.

This again helps people to find them on the internet.

Edit Metadata Tags

Use arrow keys (or ENTER key after editing) to navigate fields.

Tag	Value
Artist Name	Partakers
Track Title	Partakers Bible Thought 5 June 2022 - Pentecost Sunday
Album Title	Partakers Podcasts
Track Number	20220605
Year	2022
Genre	Bible Thought
Comments	Acts 1:8-2:2 Pentecost! The Holy Spirit Comes!
Subtitle	Acts 1:8-2:2

Add   Remove   Clear

Genres   Template

Edit...   Reset...   Load...   Save...   Set Default

☐ Don't show this when exporting audio

OK   Cancel   ?

Here is an example for the Meta Tags you can associate with each of your Podcast files.

Practise recording. It is easier than you first think.

Everyone has to start somewhere!

Have fun!

Don't be afraid to make mistakes as you learn and practise!

You will soon get into a routine.

5. The Podcast Itself

Fantabulous, Davo!

What kind of content can I put there?

Podcast about something you are passionate about and let that passion be seen in your Podcast.

Also have a clear ending, including and invitation to your listener to subscribe to your Podcast channel and keep returning.

Best length for your Podcast is between 5 and 10 minutes.

Though if you want to be longer or shorter than that, go for it! It is up to you.

Though if you want to be longer or shorter than that, go for it!

It is up to you. All your choice!

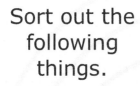

Sort out the following things.

The better prepared you are, the better, of course.

If you need help, ask somebody.

Plenty of people online willing to help for free.

Remember, every Podcaster has to start somewhere!

Next question.

What is your
Podcast name?

You need
a name
for your
Podcast!

Choose a name
which is
memorable and
give you
satisfaction.

Now get yourself some cover art. Make sure it complies to your Podcast Hosts requirement.

Here is a sample to give you some idea.

In this case, the podcast of davegroberts.podbean.com

which is forwarded to the internet address partakers.co.uk

Partakers Podcasts

Daily podcasts to help you follow Jesus Christ.

davegroberts.podbean.com / partakers.co.uk

6. Upload The Joy

Now we can weave some internet web magic!

Are you ready, Alphy?

Once you have the file ready and uploaded, you start to create a new episode on your Podcast Host.

It will look something like this.

June 5, 2022

Partakers Bible Thought 5 June 2022 - Pentecost Sunday

5 June 2022
The Holy Spirit Comes

G'day! Today is Pentecost Sunday where Christians around the world remember and celebrate the coming of the promised Holy Spirit! Happy Pentecost!

Jesus has now ascended back to the right hand of the Father. The 12 apostles are now back in Jerusalem and waiting. Waiting for the Holy Spirit to come. The coming of God the Holy Spirit is in fulfilment of the promise that Almighty and All-powerful God would indwell all those people who chose to follow Him. This event was prophesied many years before. An example is from the prophet Ezekiel:

> "And I will put my Spirit in you and move you to follow my decrees and be careful to keep my laws." (Ezekiel 36:27)

Throughout His earthly ministry Jesus had talked about how after He departed that God the Holy Spirit would come (John 15:26). Starting today and over the coming few days we will look at the Holy Spirit and into the book of Acts seeing how the Holy Spirit worked within and through the early Church. Let's look together!

Click or tap here to download this podcasts as a mp3

7. Distribute The Joy

Setup your social networks, such as Facebook and Twitter.

They will then automatically pick up your podcast which will distribute them to your friends and contacts on their platforms.

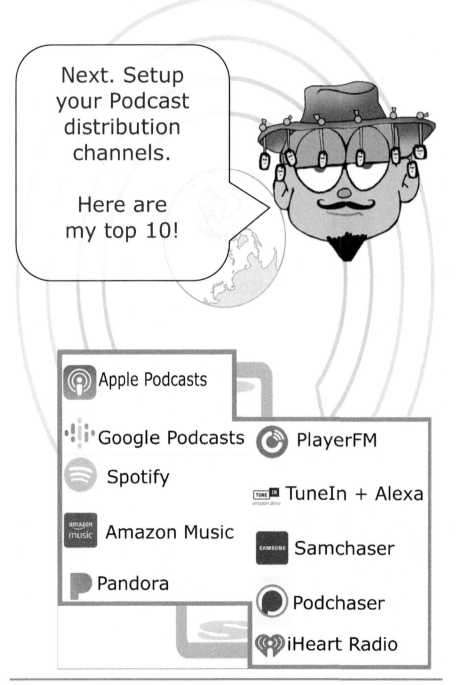

That looks good! Seems like it's a lot of hard work to do for each Podcast I release though!

Ah well, fear not, lil Alphy buddy.

Once set up on your Podcast hosting platform, its bonza and set up till you change it again!

8. Some Ideas to Podcast

Last question now.
I promise,
Drongo.

Sure thing,
me lil Rev'
Cat.
Go for it.

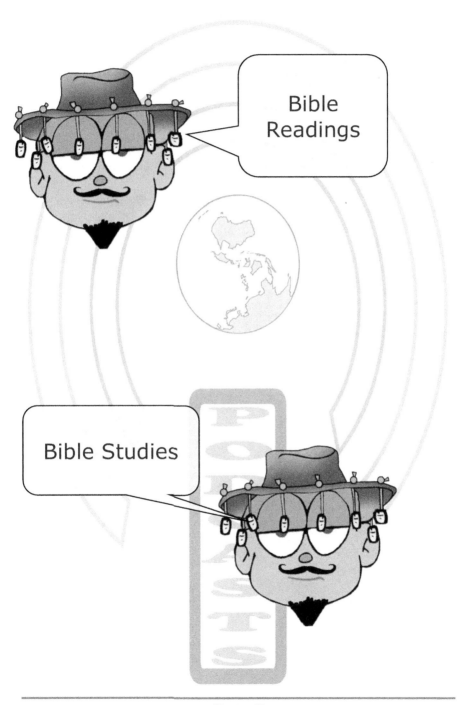

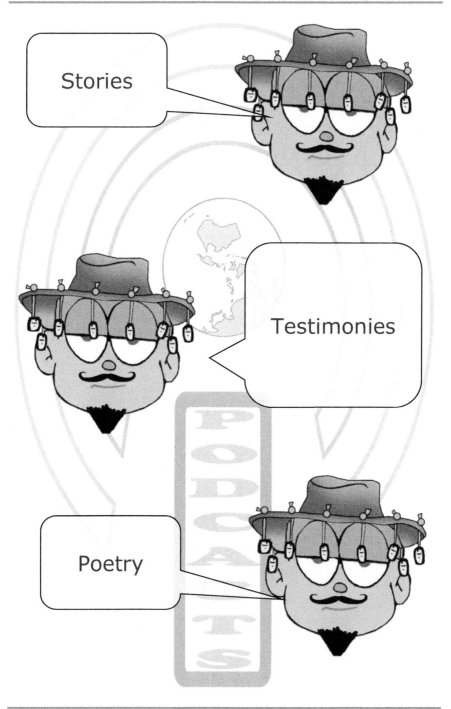

Other PulpTheology Books

AGOG: A Glimpse of God

An Ambassador in God's Orchestra of Joy

Dear Christian – Get A Good Grip

Dear Church: Wake up!

Easter Essentials: Exploring Easter

Exploring The Bible

God Gets His Hands Dirty

God, Internet Church & You

Helping the Forgotten Church

Heroes And Heretics Abound

Intimacy with God: The Devotional Life

Living Life Right: Studies in Romans 12

Scriptural Delights: Exploring Psalm 119

When Love Hits Town

WOW Words of the Bible

Glimpses Into Series:

Leviticus: A Book Of Joy

1 & 2 Chronicles: Books of heritage And history

Psalms: A Book Of Life

Song Of Songs: A Book Of Relationship

Ezekiel: A Book Of Symbols And Visions.

The Gospels: Books Of Good News

Acts: A Book Of Action

Romans: A Book Of Freedom

Read This Book Series:

Volume 1: God Of The Bible

Volume 2: Jesus Christ

Volume 3: Being A Christian

Volume 4: The Church

Volume 5: Evangelism

Volume 6: The Christian Devotional Life

Other "What's It All About, Alphy" Books

The Lord's Prayer

The Surprise of Grace (Romans 5)

Christian In Days Of Challenge (Romans 8)

Spiritual Armour

Mary and the Magnificat

All books are available in Paperback and Kindle at:

PulpTheology.co.uk

PulpTheology.com

And all Amazon sites

About The Author

I was born in a small country town in Australia. I was raised to be a sceptical agnostic/atheist with the words "Churches are dangerous places" ringing in my ears. Coming into my teenage years, I decided if Churches are so dangerous, let's rebel and go for a bit of danger. So I rebelled, became a Christian, started attending a local Christian youth group and was baptized.

In 1990, I came to the UK for 6 months' travel around Europe. Or so I thought. I have stayed ever since. I view it as God having a sense of humour. He knows I don't like rain, cold and in particular – together. He has even given me the most beautiful of women as a wife, but she doesn't like hot weather. God sure has a sense of humour.

In 2003, I had a stroke, and I took redundancy from my job. I went off to Moorlands College where I graduated in

2007 with a BA in Applied Theology. Later that year, I set up Partakers. We are now listened to in more than 100 countries a year. I have also shown many people how to do this for themselves.

I currently reside with my wife in Bournemouth in the UK. I hope you have enjoyed this book and perhaps learnt something afresh or as a reminder. Please do contact me if I need clarification concerning something here.

Peace and blessings.

About Partakers

Vision Statement: Partakers exists to communicate and distribute resources for the Christian Discipleship, Evangelism and Worship by employing radical and relevant methods, including virtual reality and online distribution.

Mission Statement: To help the world, one person at a time, to engage in whole life discipleship, as Partakers of Jesus Christ.

Contact us to see how we can help you. Seminars, coaching, preaching, teaching, discipleship or evangelism – offline or online.

Email: dave@partakers.co.uk

Mobile: 0794 794 5511

Website: http://www.partakers.co.uk

Printed in Great Britain
by Amazon

23255234R00051